I Wouldn't
Thank You for
a Valentine

I Wouldn't Thank You for a Valentine

POEMS FOR YOUNG FEMINISTS

Edited by
Carol Ann Duffy

Illustrated by Trisha Rafferty

Henry Holt and Company · *New York*

Henry Holt and Company, LLC / *Publishers since 1866*
175 Fifth Avenue / New York, New York 10010
www.henryholtchildrensbooks.com

Henry Holt® is a registered trademark of Henry Holt and Company, LLC.
This collection copyright © 1992 by Carol Ann Duffy
Illustrations copyright © 1992 by Trisha Rafferty
All rights reserved.
Originally published in Great Britain in 1992
by Viking Children's Books, the Penguin Group.

Library of Congress Cataloging-in-Publication Data
I wouldn't thank you for a valentine: poems for young feminists /
edited by Carol Ann Duffy; illustrated by Trisha Rafferty.
p.   cm.
Includes index.
Summary: A collection of poems by women from different
cultures and backgrounds, portraying the varied facets of the
female experience from childhood to old age.
1. Feminism – Juvenile poetry. 2. Young adult poetry – Women
authors. 3. Children's poetry – Women authors. [1. Feminism – Poetry.
2. Poetry – Collections.] I. Duffy, Carol Ann. II. Rafferty, Trisha, ill.
PN6109.97W68   1993   808.81'9352042 – dc20   93-3172

ISBN-13: 978-0805-05545-0
ISBN-10: 0-8050-5545-2

First American hardcover edition, 1993 by Henry Holt and Company
First American paperback edition, 1997

Printed in the United States of America on acid-free paper. ∞
5 7 9 11 13 15 14 12 10 8 6

Contents

Valentine

Not a red rose or a satin heart.

I give you an onion.
It is a moon wrapped in brown paper.
It promises light
like the careful undressing of love.

Here.
It will blind you with tears
like a lover.
It will make your reflection
a wobbling photo of grief.

I am trying to be truthful.

Not a cute card or a kissogram.

I give you an onion.
Its fierce kiss will stay on your lips,
possessive and faithful
as we are,
for as long as we are.

Take it.
Its platinum loops shrink to a wedding-ring,
if you like.

Lethal.
Its scent will cling to your fingers,
cling to your knife.

Carol Ann Duffy

For an Unborn Baby

If she's a girl,
I hope she'll stretch her wings
and grow up free, wide ranging
like a seagull, dealing with the winds
competently, swifting on currents of air,
able to live on anything she can find
in the murky sea, or even on rubbish heaps,
adapting with ease when storms drive her inland.
May she choose wisely if in the end
she settles on one name, one piece of ground.

May she banish those who'd seek to protect her
from heartbreak, or joy.
— And may he achieve no less
if he's a boy.

Janet Shepperson

Lullaby

Go to sleep, Mum,
I won't stop breathing
suddenly, in the night.

Go to sleep, I won't
climb out of my cot and
tumble downstairs.

Mum, I won't swallow
the pills the doctor gave you or
put hairpins in electric
sockets, just go to sleep.

I won't cry
when you take me to school and leave me:
I'll be happy with other children
my own age.

Sleep, Mum, sleep.
I won't
fall in the pond, play with matches,
run under a lorry or even consider
sweets from strangers.

No, I won't
give you a lot of lip,
not like some.

I won't sniff glue,
fail all my exams,
get myself/
my girlfriend pregnant.
I'll work hard and get a steady/
really worthwhile job.
I promise, go to sleep.

I'll never forget
to drop in/phone/write
and if
I need any milk, I'll yell.

Rosemary Norman

Before the Fall

After the bath with ragged towels
my Dad
would dry us very carefully:
six little wriggly girls,
each with foamy pigtails,
two rainy legs,
the invisible back we couldn't reach,
a small wet heart,
and toes, ten each.

He dried us all
the way he gave the parish
Morning Prayer:
as if it was important,
as if God was fair,
as if it was really simple
if you would just be still
and bare.

Rachel McAlpine

from Welsh Espionage

Welsh was the mother tongue, English was his.
He taught her the body by fetishist quiz,
father and daughter on the bottom stair:
'Dy benelin yw *elbow*, dy wallt di yw *hair*,

chin yw ên di, *head* yw dy ben.'
She promptly forgot, made him do it again.
Then he folded her *dwrn* and, calling it *fist*,
held it to show her *knuckles* and *wrist*.

'Let's keep it from Mam, as a special surprise.
Lips yw gwefusau, llygaid yw *eyes*.'
Each part he touched in their secret game
thrilled as she whispered its English name.

The mother was livid when she was told.
'We agreed, no English till four years old!'
She listened upstairs, her head in a whirl.
Was it such a bad thing to be Daddy's girl?

Gwyneth Lewis

School Report

'TOO EASILY SATISFIED. SPELLING STILL
 POOR.
HER GRAMMAR'S ERRATIC. LACKS CARE.
WOULD SUCCEED IF SHE WORKED.
 INCLINED TO BE SMUG.'
I think that's a wee bit unfare.

Ah well, their it is! Disappointing perhaps,
For a mum what has always had brane,
But we can't all have looks or be good at our
books . . .
She's her father all over agane.

Carole Paine

Loch, Black Rock, Beautiful Boat

'The loch, the black rock,
the beautiful boat' – these are
the names my father gave me,
brought from his boyhood
haunts in Old Caledonia.
No other that I knew had
so many names, or such a dad.
He was my poet, my eccentric
playmate, with no peer in any
kingdom anywhere. The ladies
loved him, pronouncing him
'a fine, upstanding man',
and Mother of course agreed –
and, oh, what trouble it caused!
I lost out, somehow,
in the tussle for his affections.
Seventy-seven he is now, and
nothing has changed – except
that it matters to me more than ever
that he gave me those names –
'Aline, dubh sgeir, fearr bata . . .
the loch, the black rock,
the beautiful boat.'

Meg Campbell

Indian Children Speak

People said, 'Indian children are hard to teach.
Don't expect them to talk.'
One day stubby little Boy said,
'Last night the moon went all the way with me,
When I went out to walk.'
People said, 'Indian children are very silent.
Their only words are no and yes.'
But, ragged Pansy confided softly,
'My dress is old, but at night the moon is kind;
Then I wear a beautiful moon-coloured dress.'
People said, 'Indian children are dumb.
They seldom make a reply.'
Clearly I hear Delores answer,
'Yes, the sunset is so good, I think God is throwing
A bright shawl around the shoulders of the sky.'

People said, 'Indian children have no affection.
They just don't care for anyone.'
Then I feel Ramon's hand and hear him whisper,
'A wild animal races in me since my mother sleeps
Under the ground. Will it always run and run?'
People said, 'Indian children are rude.
They don't seem very bright.'
Then I remember Joe Henry's remark,
'The tree is hanging down her head because the sun
Is staring at her. White people always stare.
They do not know it is not polite.'
People said, 'Indian children never take you in,
Outside their thoughts you'll always stand.'
I have forgotten the idle words that people said,
But treasure the day when iron doors swung wide,
And I slipped into the heart of Indian Land.

Juanita Bell

natural high

my mother is a
red
woman

she
gets high
on clean children

grows
common sense

injects
tales
with heroines

fumes
over dirty habits

hits the sky
on bad lines

cracking meteors

 my mother
gets red
with the sun

Jean Binta Breeze

Happy Birthday from Bennigans

Why did you do it, Mother?
I told you – didn't I – that I'd go with you
to a restaurant for my birthday
on one condition: Don't go and blab
to the waitress it's my BIG DAY.
But you had to go and tell her.
God, what if somebody had seen me?
I realize that you and Daddy
simply do not care if you ruin my reputation.
I almost thought for a teensy second
you had restrained yourself for once.
But no. You and your big mouth.
'Hip, hop, happy, b, birth, day,
hap, hap, happy, Happy Birthday to You!':
a zero girl, singing a zero song
at the top of her nothingness of a voice.
'All of us at Bennigans hope it's a special day!'
All of them, Mother, not just some.
That's IT for birthdays from now on.
Next year I'll be celebrating by myself.

Julie O'Callaghan

Her First Toy

I thank you for saving her life
my child
I really do
But did you have to give her
as her first toy
a white
doll

You think I am insincere
ungrateful
incapable of thanking you
But at this time
There is nothing big enough
to wipe away our difference
There is nothing
to bring us together
which does not leave a scar
the wounds as you see
are gaping

I thank you for saving her life
my child
I really do
But I wish you did not give her
as her first toy
a white
doll.

Sylvia Parker

Latch-key Child

Closing the door of the empty house
she puts on her skates
and inherits again the cold wild pavements.

Her metal wheels whiten the paving stones
but the skidmarks show only behind her eyes

Sometimes across hours of cold air
she sees boys on bikes,
flocks of orphaned birds

and she joins them,
the lost migration
arcing over and over the sunless streets.

Sometimes one is lost to the burning shriek of rubber
sirens, or the shrill hands of adults.
Sometimes one is lost to the sweetshop,
the comics, the black shine of hell's angels.

But always someone is left to ride with,
to run against the wind, the darkening of the sun,
to sleep with eyes open on cold cushions of air,
to run the relay with no message, no baton

Only to not know that a door is closed
that a room is empty
that a voice can walk faster than light

and a sherbet lemon and a gobstopper
do not last very long.

Valerie Sinason

school days

one day
the school bus
missed its turning
crushed our mate
against the gate
doctor gave us tablets
for our nerves

the school choir
sang
at the funeral
a man looked at me
like a ghost
he had heard it was
the brown-skinned one

Jean Binta Breeze

Vestment

Sometimes in the morning
I wake up frozen
And, still half asleep,
I pull, drowsy and shivering,
My young, warm, silky
Body over myself.
I wrap myself in it
Teeth chattering childishly,
Happy that for one more day,
One whole day
I will be
In a shelter from eternity.

Ana Blandiana
(Translated from the
Romanian by Peter Jay &
Anca Cristofovici)

A Happy Childhood

I used to enjoy peeling oranges
keeping the skin intact.

I used to enjoy picking over rice
throwing out the husks.

I used to enjoy polishing the slatted floor
with a coconut-hair brush,
until it shone in my face.

I used to enjoy running to Chino's
to collect hot toast in brown paper
for supper with cocoa or herb tea.

There were oranges in abundance,
whole sackfuls of rice.
My home was a contented one
and Chino's home to fiestas.

My childhood was happy, happy.
I had hardworking hands,
and was filled with hope.

Eulalia Bernard
(Translated by Amanda Hopkinson)

Grown Up

Bored by the day,
I decided I'd do something
I hadn't done in years —
go outside and play.
I tried to remember
jump-rope games,
the rules of hide-and-seek,
did you count to forty or a hundred?

I went out and attempted to act naturally.
I hummed a little and kicked a stone
down the street looking for other kids.
They were playing hopscotch.
I showed them marbles
and penny candy and dominoes.
They stared up at me like lilliputians
and said I was too old.

Julie O'Callaghan

Accomplishments

I painted a picture – green sky – and showed it to my
   mother.
She said that's nice, I guess.
So I painted another holding the paintbrush in my
   teeth,
Look, Ma, no hands. And she said
I guess someone would admire that if they knew
How you did it and they were interested in painting
   which I am not.

I played clarinet solo in Gounod's Clarinet Concerto
With the Buffalo Philharmonic. Mother came to listen
   and said
That's nice, I guess.
So I played it with the Boston Symphony,
Lying on my back and using my toes,
Look, Ma, no hands. And she said
I guess someone would admire that if they knew
How you did it and they were interested in music
   which I am not.

I made an almond soufflé and served it to my mother.
She said that's nice, I guess.
So I made another, beating it with my breath,
Serving it with my elbows,
Look, Ma, no hands. And she said
I guess someone would admire that if they knew
How you did it and they were interested in eating
   which I am not.

So I sterilized my wrists, performed the amputation, threw away
My hands and went to my mother, but before I could say
Look, Ma, no hands, she said
I have a present for you and insisted I try on
The blue kid-gloves to make sure they were the right size.

Cynthia MacDonald

The Name of the Game

'Catch the *ball!*' the teacher cried.
I ran, I jumped, I stretched, I tried.
I really did.
    – I missed.

'Useless!' she yelled. 'Silly girl!' she spat.
'What on earth d'you think you're playing at?'
'A game,' I said.
    – And wept.

Jenny Craig

shopping

look over there in that window
isn't that lovely
the sort of thing that would
go with your hair
it would look nice on you

we'll go & try it on
shall we?
well, all right. perhaps not
a bit saggy in the neck

well. what about this one?
i've told you before
i haven't got money to throw away
on rubbish

i don't like that
you know that kind of thing
looks terrible with your shoulders

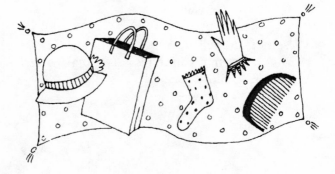

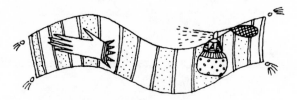

you don't want that.
that's not what we're looking for.
you've several of those already.

what about this?
in another colour?
if they have it in your size.

i won't throw money away.
i've told you. no. no. no.
definitely not.
i don't care who else is wearing them

i can't understand
why you're so difficult
to please

Jenny Boult

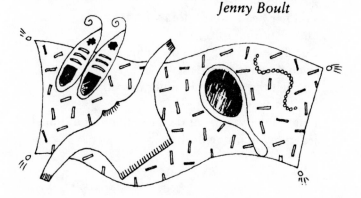

Sally

She was a dog-rose kind of girl:
elusive, scattery as petals;
scratchy sometimes, tripping you like briars.
She teased the boys
turning this way and that, not to be tamed
or taught any more than the wind.
Even in school the word 'ought'
had no meaning for Sally.
On dull days
she'd sit quiet as a mole at her desk
delving in thought.
But when the sun called
she was gone, running the blue day down
till the warm hedgerows prickled the dusk
and moths flickered out.

Her mother scolded; Dad
gave the hazel-switch,
said her head was stuffed with feathers
and a starling tongue.
But they couldn't take the shine out of her.
Even when it rained
you felt the sun saved under her skin.
She'd a way of escape
laughing at you from the bright end of a tunnel,
leaving you in the dark.

Phoebe Hesketh

Peck's Bad Boys

Teacher called me a *hussy*.
I told her I just wanted to be one of the guys.
Their games more daring, longer-lasting
like an all-day sucker.
Not fighting exactly
no back-biting, hair-pulling,
just out-front shin-kicking, punching
wrestling in the dirt.
Rolling, maybe laughing.
I told her I just liked the contact
all that hard muscle,
all those smells, dust, sweat, warm flesh.

Judi Benson

Good Girls

Good girls
will always go like clockwork
home from school,

through the iron gates
where clambering boys
whisper and pull,

past houses
where curtains twitch
and a fingery witch beckons,

by the graveyard
where stone angels stir,
itching their wings,

past tunnelled woods
where forgotten wolves wait
for prey,

past dens
and caves and darknesses
they go like clockwork;

and when they come
to school again
their homework's done.

Irene Rawnsley

Don't Smack Me Again

Tomato hurt.
Tomato tight in hurt skin.
Hurt tomato red with held breath.
Red hurt tomato held tight in skin.
Hurt breath red with tomato.
Tight hurt tomato red.
Red skin in hurt tomato.
Held red tight with hurt breath.
Skin tomato tight with hurt held.
Hurt skin tight with tomato.
Hurt tomato.

Deborah Randall

This Cat

This cat
she expects love.
Demands it
stalks it
feels she has a right to it.
She is not ashamed –
I wish I were more like this cat.

Gabriela Pearse

Advice to a Teenage Daughter

You have found a new war-game
called Love.
Here on your dressing-table
stand arrayed
brave ranks of lipsticks
brandishing
swords of cherry pink and flame.
Behold the miniature armies
of little jars,
packed with the scented
dynamite of flowers.
See the dreaded tweezers;
tiny pots
of manufactured moonlight,
stick-on stars.
Beware my sweet;
conquest may seem easy
but you can't compete with football,
motor cycles, cars,
cricket, computer-games,
or a plate of chips.

Isobel Thrilling

Thirteen

All summer she twirled
in pearls and satin gowns,
pale as a mushroom
in the dark attic.
Sometimes her aunt or
her father would hint that
the field of Queen Anne's lace
at the end of the road
was chock-full of children
her age. Her age
was suddenly uncertain as
the moon of breath
waxing and waning
in an oxygen tent
all summer long.
Nothing to do but wait.
In the stale heat
of the attic, in the rippled
full-length mirror,
she posed
in velvet, in chiffon,
in her mother's useless clothes:
waiting for her breasts
to blossom and fill
the loose bodice of her grief.

Julie Kane

Hanging Fire

I am fourteen
and my skin has betrayed me
the boy I cannot live without
still sucks his thumb
in secret
how come my knees are
always so ashy
what if I die
before morning
and momma's in the bedroom
with the door closed.

I have to learn how to dance
in time for the next party
my room is too small for me
suppose I die before graduation
they will sing sad melodies
but finally
tell the truth about me
There is nothing I want to do
and too much
that has to be done
and momma's in the bedroom
with the door closed.

Nobody even stops to think
about my side of it
I should have been on Math Team
my marks were better than his
why do I have to be
the one
wearing braces
I have nothing to wear tomorrow
will I live long enough
to grow up
and momma's in the bedroom
with the door closed.

Audre Lorde

Turning Sixteen

Always cycling.
Always wearing odd clothes
sent from America or passed down.
Summer dresses make the best wear.
In winter I have one good coat
and one for hacking.

The town girls have the latest,
faded jeans, jazzy tops.
They smoke too, on the hill to school.
I am better than that.
I smoke in my private room.

I must have the biggest arse in school,
flopping like unmoulded jelly.
My face is a tomato
when I am asked to speak.
My hair is always tossed.

There must be a secret.
Are they never cold,
must wear caps and flatten their hair?
How are their legs so brown?

How can I be a film-star
with my scar
and my yellow teeth
and my phlegmy throat?

Máighréad Medbh

Bette Davis

Maybe it's really Bette Davis I want
to be the good twin or even better the bad
one or a nanny who drowns a baby in a bath
I'm not sure maybe I'd prefer Katharine
Hepburn tossing my red hair, having a hot
temper. I says to my teacher *Can't I be
Elizabeth Taylor*, drunk and fat and she
just laughed, not much of a chance of that.
I went for an audition for *The Prime
of Miss Jean Brodie*. I didn't get a part
even though I've been acting longer
than Beverley Innes. So I have. Honest.

Jackie Kay

33

Aunt Leaf

Needing one, I invented her –
the great-great-aunt dark as hickory
called Shining-Leaf, or Drifting-Cloud
or The-Beauty-of-the-Night.

Dear aunt, I'd call into the leaves,
and she'd rise up, like an old log in a pool,
and whisper in a language only the two of us knew
the word that meant *follow*,

and we'd travel
cheerful as birds
out of the dusty town and into the trees
where she would change us both into something
    quicker –
two foxes with black feet,
two snakes green as ribbons,
two shimmering fish –
and all day we'd travel.

At day's end she'd leave me back at my own door
with the rest of my family,
who were kind, but solid as wood
and rarely wandered. While she,
old twist of feathers and birch bark,
would walk in circles wide as rain and then
float back

scattering the rags of twilight
on fluttering moth wings;

or she'd slouch from the barn like a grey opossum;

or she'd hang in the milky moonlight
burning like a medallion,

this bone dream,
this friend I had to have,
this old woman made out of leaves.

Mary Oliver

The Nature Lesson

The teacher has the flowers on her desk,
Then goes round, giving one to each of us.
We are going to study the primrose –
To find out all about it. It has five petals,
Notice the little dent in each, making it heart-shaped
And a pale green calyx (And O! the hairy stem!).
Now, in the middle of the flower
There may be a little knob – that is the pistil –
Or perhaps your flower may show the bunch of
     stamens.
               We look at our flowers
To find out which kind we have got.

Now we are going to look inside,
So pull your petals off, one by one.
               But wait . . .
If I pull my flower to pieces it will stop
Being a primrose. It will be just bits
Strewn on my desk. I can't pull it to pieces.
What does it matter what goes on inside?
I won't find out by pulling it to pieces,
Because it will not be a primrose any more,
And the bits will not mean anything at all.
A primrose is a primrose, not just bits.

It lies there, a five-petalled primrose,
A whole primrose, a living primrose.
To find out what is inside I make it dead,
And then it will not be a primrose.
              You can't find out
What goes on inside a living flower that way.
The teacher talks, fingers rustle . . .
I will look over my neighbour's flower
And leave my primrose whole. But if the teacher comes
And tells me singly to pull my flower to pieces
Then I will do as I am told. The teacher comes,
Passes my neighbour on her gangway side,
Does not see my primrose is still whole,
Goes by, not noticing; nobody notices.

My flower remains a primrose, that they all
Want to find out about by pulling to pieces.
I am alone: all the world is alone
In the flower left breathing on my desk.

Marjorie Baldwin

The Royal Grammar School, Newcastle

The R.G.S. make me sick.
They wear a black uniform, from the third year on;
In the sixth form they change to grey.
Then they leave and join a bank.

Elaine Cusack

Short Thought

I wish I had rings running through me like trees,
Then you'd know I wasn't lying about my age.

Elaine Cusack

Piccadilly Line

Girls, dressed for dancing,
board the tube at Earls Court,
flutter, settle.
Chattering, excited by a vision
of glitter, their fragile bodies
carry invisible antennae,
missing nothing.
Faces velvet with bright camouflage,
they're unsung stars – so young
it's thrilling just to be away from home.

One shrieks, points, springs away.
She's seen a moth
caught up in the blonde strands
of her companion's hair,
a moth, marked
with all the shadow colours of blonde.
The friend's not scared;
gently, she shakes her head,
tumbles it, dead,
into her hands.

At Piccadilly Circus they take flight,
skimming the escalator,
brushing past the collector,
up to the lure of light.

Carole Satyamurti

Skanking Englishman Between Trains

Met him at Birmingham Station
small yellow hair Englishman
hi-fi stereo swinging in one hand
walking in rhythm to reggae sound/Man

he was alive
he was full-o-jive
said he had a lovely
Jamaican wife

Said he couldn't remember
the taste of English food
I like mih drops
me johnny cakes
me peas and rice
me soup/ Man

he was alive
he was full-o-jive
said he had a lovely
Jamaican wife

Said, showing me her photo,
whenever we have a little quarrel
you know/ to sweeten her up
I surprise her with a nice mango/Man

he was alive
he was full-o-jive
said he had a lovely Jamaican wife

Grace Nichols

40

Self-portraits

The cupboard contains my dresses, the drawer my
    faces.
Seven selves lie on seven shelves.

I try them on every night, a concoction of fig-leaves
To cover all possible cases. I am Juliet,
Cleopatra, Marilyn – everyone, except naked
Susanna Smith, my mother and father's daughter.

I owe nobody the make of my body.
I bought myself at Boots – the cosmetic counter
And the slimming aids. I shopped for myself in
    windows
And women's magazines, and then in the long, long
    mirrors
In the eyes of the watchers of birds.

I twist my mouth in the glass. I peer anxiously,
And erase, and alter – the artist after perfection
With pencil and brush, the ladies' do-it-yourself
Portable Rembrandt, the only self-portrait that has to
Be painted afresh every morning.
                            Nice work, in its way –
Not boring, certainly, the supple capacity
To make oneself up as one goes, to carry the light
And rainbow style of continuous creation

But I like myself best in the bath, where it all comes
    off.

Elma Mitchell

For Heidi with Blue Hair

When you dyed your hair blue
(or, at least, ultramarine
for the clipped sides, with a crest
of jet-black spikes on top)
you were sent home from school

because, as the headmistress put it,
although dyed hair was not
specifically forbidden, yours
was, apart from anything else,
not done in the school colours.

Tears in the kitchen, telephone-calls
to school from your freedom-loving father:
'She's not a punk in her behaviour;
it's just a style.' (You wiped your eyes,
also not in a school colour.)

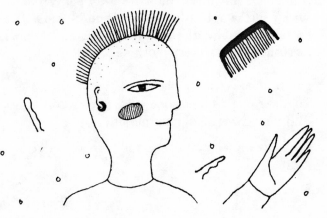

'She discussed it with me first –
we checked the rules.' 'And anyway, Dad,
it cost twenty-five dollars.
Tell them it won't wash out – not even if I
    wanted to try.'

It would have been unfair to mention
your mother's death, but that
shimmered behind the arguments.
The school had nothing else against you;
the teachers twittered and gave in.

Next day your black friend had hers done
in grey, white and flaxen yellow –
the school colours precisely:
an act of solidarity, a witty
tease. The battle was already won.

Fleur Adcock

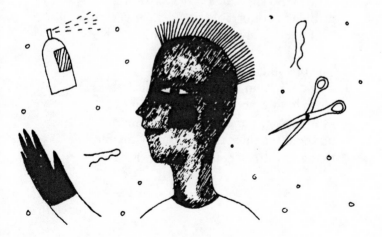

43

Sex, Politics and Religion

Her features unfold as she lowers her head
back against the basin. I play for time,
getting the temperature of the water just right.
I have almost grown used to touching old hair
and have learnt to respect a customer's face,
clamping my free hand against the forehead

and forcing the spray tight against the scalp.
I must keep my eyes on my fingers
and must not stare at her feathery cheeks
or the rolling chin that falls away to reveal
her puckered throat and the seamless hole
through which she now has to breathe.

If I understood the words burped into shape
by her new oesophageal voice, I might
ask about cancer and what would happen
if my hand slipped and the harsh foam
dribbled comfortably down a network of gullies,
or if a fly . . . I have to get a look.

The opening is neat and dark,
framed by skin of an unbearable softness.
She has shut her eyes and is smiling
as I massage hard and keep my mind
on the three things I was told by my mother
that a hairdresser should never discuss.

Lavinia Greenlaw

Phenomenal Woman

Pretty women wonder where my secret lies.
I'm not cute or built to suit a fashion model's size
But when I start to tell them,
They think I'm telling lies.
I say,
It's in the reach of my arms,
The span of my hips,
The stride of my step,
The curl of my lips.
I'm a woman
Phenomenally.
Phenomenal woman,
That's me.

I walk into a room
Just as cool as you please,
And to a man,
The fellows stand or
Fall down on their knees.
Then they swarm around me,
A hive of honey bees.
I say,
It's the fire in my eyes,
And the flash of my teeth,
The swing in my waist,
And the joy in my feet.
I'm a woman
Phenomenally.
Phenomenal woman,
That's me.

Men themselves have wondered
What they see in me.
They try so much
But they can't touch
My inner mystery.
When I try to show them
They say they still can't see.
I say,
It's in the arch of my back,
The sun of my smile,
The ride of my breasts,
The grace of my style.
I'm a woman
Phenomenally.
Phenomenal woman,
That's me.

Now you understand
Just why my head's not bowed.
I don't shout or jump about
Or have to talk real loud.
When you see me passing
It ought to make you proud.
I say,
It's in the click of my heels,
The bend of my hair,
The palm of my hand,
The need for my care.
'Cause I'm a woman
Phenomenally.
Phenomenal woman,
That's me.

Maya Angelou

Blind Girl

I take your hand. I want to touch your eyes.
They are water soft. I know. I could push them in.
Once a doll's eyes fell in before my fingers –
Instead of dropping tick-tock open and shut
They were cold holes like a poor frozen faucet.
Where does the water come from? I hear breathing.
Listen at the tap – you hear a kind of sobbing.

But your eyes have a panting kind of hush
And then a shudder like a huddled bird's
Lifting his neck-feathers in my two cupped hands.
That's the light in them, asking to get let out.
(Your lashes beat and beat against my fingers.)
And when we walk together, heat on my shoulders
Is soft as down, and that's a light called outside.

So seeing is something struggling to get out
To something like it, larger but more still,
And when you see, that must feel just like swimming.
I take your hand. There. Please let me hold you.
If I hold tight enough to your live fingers
It *must* work free. Oh, I could kill your eyes
Only to know a little more what sight is.

Jane Cooper

Disabled Swimmers' Night

I would get given that one.
Bean-bag body,
dribbling,
arms jerking.
I know she can't help it
but it gives me the creeps.
Help her in a minute,
just a bit longer,
chatting.

Any minute, I'll be fish,
dizzy, jazzy, snazzy
water dancer.
I'll be blade
slicing great arcs
flashing silver.
Bird – swift
swooping through blue . . .
please let him help me. Now.

I hear her snuffling,
shouting, her hand
grabs at my wrist.
Panic. I want to push her,
get away. But say
'you fancy me then, darling?'
winking at the others.
We laugh; the moment passes.
Don't suppose she noticed.

Carole Satyamurti

Please Give This Seat to
an Elderly or Disabled Person

I stood during the entire journey:
nobody offered me a seat
although I was at least a hundred years older than
   anyone else on board,
although the signs of at least three major afflictions
were visible on me:
Pride, Loneliness, and Art.

Nina Cassian
(Translated from the Romanian by Naomi Lazard)

Didactica Nova

How many fingers have you got on one hand?
Five, replied the child.
So, how many do five and five make?
Eleven, comes the answer.
Can you blame me for getting cross with you?
Didn't I say count?
Why can't you understand
And answer like all the rest!
What if everyone answered like that?
What would happen if nobody understood?
How many fingers have you got on one hand?
Five, replied the child.
Well, how many on two hands?
Eleven, comes the answer.
The blows fall. On the hand with five fingers,
On the hand
        with six.

Grete Tartler
(Translated by Andrea Deletant &
Brenda Walker)

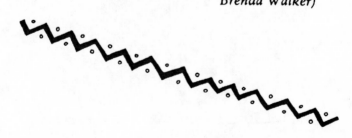

I am Happy

Today I have discovered happiness.
Today I learnt
it's not that I'm *on* the way
         or *by* the way
         or *with* the way
I *am* the way!

Delfy Gochez Fernandez
(Translated by Amanda Hopkinson)

Remember

Remember?

Remember me?
I am the girl
with the dark skin
whose shoes are thin
I am the girl
with rotted teeth
I am the dark
rotten-toothed girl
with the wounded eye
and the melted ear.

I am the girl
holding their babies
cooking their meals
sweeping their yards
washing their clothes
Dark and rotting
and wounded, wounded.

I would give
to the human race
only hope.

53

I am the woman
with the blessed
dark skin
I am the woman
with teeth repaired
I am the woman
with the healing eye
the ear that hears.

I am the woman: Dark,
repaired, healed
Listening to you.

I would give
to the human race
only hope.

I am the woman
offering two flowers
whose roots
are twin

Justice and Hope

Let us begin.

Alice Walker

The Class Game

How can you tell what class I'm from?
I can talk posh like some
With an 'Olly in me mouth
Down me nose, wear an 'at not a scarf
With me second-hand clothes.
So why do you always wince when you hear
Me say 'Tara' to me 'Ma' instead of 'Bye Mummy
    dear'?
How can you tell what class I'm from?
'Cos we live in a corpy, not like some
In a pretty little semi, out Wirral way
And commute into Liverpool by train each day?
Or did I drop my unemployment card
Sitting on your patio (We have a yard)?
How can you tell what class I'm from?
Have I a label on me head, and another on me bum?
Or is it because my hands are stained with toil?
Instead of soft lily-white with perfume and oil?
Don't I crook me little finger when I drink me tea
Say toilet instead of bog when I want to pee?
Why do you care what class I'm from?
Does it stick in your gullet like a sour plum?
Well, mate! A cleaner is me mother
A docker is me brother
Bread pudding is wet nelly
And me stomach is me belly
And I'm proud of the class that I come from.

Mary Casey

Yuh Hear Bout?

Yuh hear bout di people dem arres
Fi bun dung di Asian people dem house?
Yuh hear bout di policeman dem lock up
Fi beat up di black bwoy widout a cause?
Yuh hear bout di MP dem sack because im
   refuse fi help
im coloured constituents in a dem fight
   'gainst deportation?
Yuj noh hear bout dem?
Me neida.

Valerie Bloom

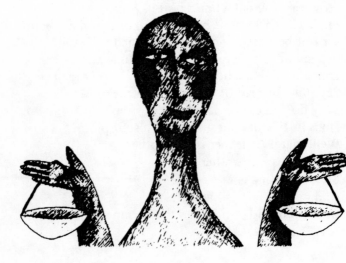

We Can Always

A television comedian says:
'Women are no longer bobbing
their hair because
they are slanting
their eyes'

and people laugh

A television comedian says:
'Hi! I'm Ruru,
fry me
to Frorida'

and people laugh

A disc jockey says:
'You should know better
than to rob
a Chinese grocer
If you do
you will want to rob
again in another hour'

and people laugh

A newspaper columnist says:
'How come them heathen
      Chinee
are always observing New Year's
a month late? When they gonna
get up to date?'

and if we can't laugh
at ourselves, we can always
go back

Nellie Wong

A Short Note on Schoolgirls

Schoolgirls are heroes –
they have so many things to pass:
exams, notes in class, hockey balls –
and great big men on building sites
who go WOOAR.

Alison Campbell

Women Laughing

Gurgles, genderless,
Inside the incurious womb.

Random soliloquies of babies
Tickled by everything.

Undomesticated shrieks
Of small girls. Mother prophesies
You'll be crying in a minute.

Adolescents wearing giggles
Like chain-mail, against embarrassment,
Giggles formal in shape as
Butterpats, or dropped stitches.

Young women anxious to please,
Laughing eagerly before the punchline
(Being too naive to know which it is).

Wives gleaming sleekly in public at
Husbandly jokes, masking
All trace of old acquaintance.

Mums obliging with rhetorical
Guffaws at the children's riddles
That bored their parents.

Old women, unmanned, free
Of children, embarrassment, desire to please,
Hooting grossly, without explanation.

U. A. Fanthorpe

Whatweakersex?

There's one thing I've always wanted to do
cos I think it'd be such fun.
It's to go round pinching every man I see
firmly on the bum.
To watch them blush and edge away
would be my greatest thrill.
On tubes and crowded pavements
I'd be out to kill.
I'd pull a hefty handful of flesh
from off their manly cheek,
or perhaps I'd try a simpler style
and perfect a gentle tweak.
Denim bums and pinstripe bums
I'd give them all fair share,
a pinch just hard enough to prove
that tweaker sex was there.

Fran Landsman

Sly Autumn

Sly Autumn
crept up my skirt
today
in Mainguard Street.

Rita Ann Higgins

You Held Out the Light

You held out the light to light my cigarette
But when I leaned down to the flame
It singed my eyebrows and my hair;
Now it is always the same – no matter where
We meet, you burn me.
I must always stop and rub my eyes
And beat the living fire from my hair.

Gwendolyn MacEwen

I Wouldn't Thank You for a Valentine

(Rap)

I wouldn't thank you for a Valentine.
I won't wake up early wondering if the postman's
  been.
Should 10 red-padded satin hearts arrive with a sticky
  sickly saccharine
Sentiments in very vulgar verses I wouldn't wonder if
  you meant them.
Two dozen anonymous Interflora roses?
I'd not bother to swither who sent them!
I wouldn't thank you for a Valentine.

Scrawl SWALK across the envelope
I'd just say 'Same Auld Story
I canny be bothered deciphering it —
I'm up to here with Amore!
The whole Valentine's Day Thing is trivial and
  commercial,
A cue for unleashing clichés and candyheart motifs to
  which I personally am not partial.'
Take more than singing telegrams, or pints of Chanel
  Five, or sweets,
To get me ordering oysters or ironing my black satin
  sheets.
I wouldn't thank you for a Valentine.

If you sent me a solitaire and promises solemn,
Took out an ad in the *Guardian* Personal Column
Saying something very soppy such as 'Who Loves Ya,
   Poo?
I'll tell you, I do, Fozzy Bear, that's who!'
You'd entirely fail to charm me, in fact I'd detest it
I wouldn't be eighteen again for anything, I'm glad I'm
   past it.
I wouldn't thank you for a Valentine.

If you sent me a single orchid, or a pair of Janet
   Reger's in a heart-shaped box and declared your
   Love Eternal
I'd say I'd not be caught dead in them they were
   politically suspect and I'd rather something thermal.
If you hired a plane and blazed our love in a banner
   across the skies;
If you bought me something flimsy in a flatteringly
   wrong size;
If you sent me a postcard with three Xs and told me
   how you felt
I wouldn't thank you, I'd melt.

Liz Lochhead

Small Words

You will complain
I was intrusive:
no more than your hands.

I read your card
to her, small words:
you wrote *all my love*.

Fiona Hall

Echo and Narcissus

When sweet Echo met Narcissus
She desired to be his missus.
But Narcissus took a dekko
At himself and not at Echo.
Now forever must he shiver
As he hovers o'er the river.
Echo too is out of luck
All she wanted was a man to love and to cherish her.

Gerda Mayer

Sweet Sixteen

Well, you can't say
they didn't try.
Mamas never mentioned menses.
A nun screamed: You vulgar girl
don't say brassières
say bracelets.
She pinned paper sleeves
on to our sleeveless dresses.
The preacher thundered:
Never go with a man alone
Never alone
and even if you're engaged
only passionless kisses.

At sixteen, Phoebe asked me:
Can it happen when you're in a dance hall
I mean, you know what,
getting *preggers* and all that, *when*
you're dancing?
I, sixteen, assured her
you could.

Eunice de Souza

Magnetic

i spell it out on this fridge door
you are so wonderful
i even like th way you snor

Wendy Cope

Song (October 1969)

I love you, Mrs Acorn. Would your husband mind
if I kissed you under the autumn sun,
if my brown-leaf guilty passion made you blind
to his manly charms and fun?

I want you, Mrs Acorn. Do you think you'll come
to see my tangled, windswept desires,
and visit me in my everchanging house of some
vision of winter's fires?

I am serious, Mrs Acorn, do you hear?
Forget your family and other ties,
come with me to where there is no fear,
where we'll find summer butterflies.

I am serious, Mrs Acorn, are you deaf?

Kath Fraser

Space-age Lover

Let me be your space-age lover,
teleporting to your bed.
In a psychical intrusion
let me reach inside your head.
I will lock-in circuits with you
for a trans-Galactic surge
in molecular abandon
as our atoms blend and merge.

In the magic fourth dimension
we will time warp up to Mars,
popping love-pills by the dozen
as we sport among the stars.
We will conquer time and motion
in the saucer-bowl of space,
and my kisses burn like lasers
as I rush you back to base.

I will lunar-bug it to you
from the mountains of the moon.
I will set your robots dancing
to an electronic croon.
I will bleep you down a sunbeam,
make the rainbow's bend unfurl,
and we'll tumble down the aeons
in a planetary whirl.

As our eyes transmit a message
in a rocket-orbit blink
we'll unzip spacesuits together
and we'll transformation-link
in a mind-exploding fusion,
love-entangled on your bed.
Let me be your space-age lover:
let me reach inside your head.

Jennifer Brice

A Simple Story

A visiting conductor
   when I was seventeen,
took me back to his hotel room
   to cover the music scene.

I'd written a composition.
   Would wonders never cease –
here was a real musician
   prepared to hold my piece.

He spread my score on the counterpane
   with classic casualness,
and put one hand on the manuscript
   and the other down my dress.

It was hot as hell in the Windsor.
   I said I'd like a drink.
We talked across gin and grapefruit,
   and I heard the ice go clink

as I gazed at the lofty forehead
   of one who led the band,
and guessed at the hoarded sorrows
   no wife could understand.

I dreamed of a soaring passion
   as an egg might dream of flight,
while he read my crude sonata.
   If he'd said, 'That bar's not right,'

or, 'Have you thought of a coda?'
   or, 'Watch that first repeat,'
or, 'Modulate to the dominant,'
   he'd have had me at his feet.

But he shuffled it all together,
   and said, 'That's *lovely*, dear,'
as he put it down on the washstand
   in a way that made it clear

that I was no composer.
   And I being young and vain,
removed my lovely body
   from one who'd scorned my brain.

I swept off like Miss Virtue
   down dusty Roma Street,
and heard the goods trains whistle
   WHO? WHOOOOOO? in aching heat.

Gwen Harwood

70

The Juggler's Wife

Last night, in front of thousands of people,
he placed a pencil on his nose
and balanced a chair upright on it
while he spun a dozen plates behind his back.
Then he slowly stood on his head to read a book
at the same time as he transferred the lot
to the big toe of his left foot.
They said it was impossible.

This morning, in our own kitchen,
I ask him to help with the washing-up –
so he gets up, knocks over a chair,
trips over the cat, swears, drops the tray
and smashes the whole blooming lot!
You wouldn't think it was possible.

Cicely Herbert

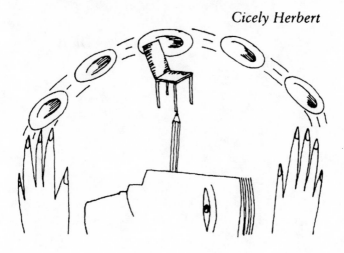

Lovesick

I found an apple.
A red and shining apple.
I took its photograph.

I hid the apple in the attic.
I opened the skylight
and the sun said *Ah*!

At night, I checked that it was safe,
under the giggling stars,
the sly moon. My cool apple.

Whatever you are calling about,
I am not interested.
Go away. You with the big teeth.

Carol Ann Duffy

Chat Show

'You never married.' 'No,' he said,
'Relationships were not my *forte*.'
'Any regrets?' 'Ah . . . ' Here we supply
the bitter-sweet accompaniment.
Of course. But he had higher ends
than procreation. Who could fill
the deep well of his genius? 'Perhaps.'

'You never married.' 'No,' she said,
'I wasn't asked.' Poor thing,
ceaselessly shovelling her work
into that lack. 'Regrets?'
'No, none at all.' Oh well, she would say that.

Vicki Raymond

To *the Spider in the Crevice*
Behind the Toilet Door

i have left you four flies
three are in the freezer next to the joint of beef
the other is wrapped in christmas paper
tied with a pink ribbon
beside the ironing-table in the hall
should you need to contact me
in an emergency
the number's in the book
by the telephone.

p.s. i love you

Janet Sutherland

A Woman's Work

Will you forgive me that I did not run
to welcome you as you came in the door?
Forgive I did not sew your buttons on
and left a mess strewn on the kitchen floor?
A woman's work is never done
and there is more.

The things I did I should have left undone
the things I lost that I could not restore;
Will you forgive I wasn't any fun?
Will you forgive I couldn't give you more?
A woman's work is never done
and there is more.

I never finished what I had begun,
I could not keep the promises I swore,
so we fought battles neither of us won
and I said 'Sorry!' and you banged the door.
A woman's work is never done
and there is more.

But in the empty space now you are gone
I find the time I didn't have before.
I lock the house and walk out to the sun
where the sea beats upon a wider shore
and woman's work is never done,
not any more.

Dorothy Nimmo

Frying Tonight

This chip shop lady
has a certain way about her:
a way of saying – 'You OK?',
a way of making a wire basket
full of chips bounce up and down
with one hand while the other
flips back her hair,
a way of snapping up a chip bag,
flicking it with two fingers to open it
and pushing her fist in to keep it open,
a way of setting out all the orders
in a neat row, of smoothing down her apron
to rid her hands of grease,
a way of making you notice
an extraordinary shade of blue
on her upper eyelid
as she bats her lashes and says, 'Is that everything,
    love?'

Julie O'Callaghan

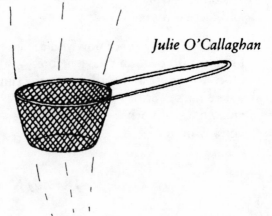

Monument

A person –
a lady –
told me,
'Always ripen
peaches
in a paper bag.'
I think of her
every time
I eat one.
All summer.
Every year.

Felice Holman

At a Cannery

The white eyes of the red-faced crabs are glaring at
  the noisy women all around them.
Day after day is a black day for crabs at the cannery.
Upon the soft bed of the conveyor-belt, they cry:
'Hey, tell me, what have they done with my hands and
  feet?'
'Hey, tell me, what have they done with my insides?'

But the women, pretending not to hear anything, work
  on,
their hands busy and tireless.

Then the white glaring eyes are thrown into a tub,
  not even allowed to say goodbye to one another.
The processed bits of crabs are sealed into the pitch
  blackness of cans
but go on crying:
'Hey, help me out! I want to go home!'

But the women are set-faced, working away on the
  torrent dashing
along the conveyor-belt, as if all they have to live for
is to despatch crabs to the tables of cultivated
  gentlemen.

Nishio Katsuko
(Translated by
James Kirkup)

The Women of Mumbles Head*

The moon is sixpence,
A pillar of salt or
A shoal of herring.
But on such a night,
Wild as the wet wind,
Larger than life,
She casts a long line
Over the slippery sea.
And the women of Mumbles Head
Are one, a long line,
Over the slippery sea.
Wet clothes clog them,
Heavy ropes tire them,
But the women of Mumbles Head
Are one, a long line,
Over the slippery sea.
And under white beams
Their strong arms glisten,
Like silver, like salt,
Like a shoal of herring,
Under the slippery sea.
And they haul
For their dear ones,
And they call
For their dear ones,
Casting a long line
Over the slippery sea.
But the mounting waves
Draw from them,

The mountain waves
Draw from them,
The bodies of their dear ones,
O, the bodies of their dear ones,
Drawn under the slippery sea.
In a chain of shawls
They hook one in,
Fish-wet, moonlit,
They've plucked him back
From under the slippery sea.
For the moon is sixpence,
A pillar of salt or
A shoal of herring,
And the women of Mumbles Head
Are one, a long line
Over the slippery sea.

Maura Dooley

*The women rescued a lifeboatman by making a rope of
their knotted shawls, after the Mumbles lifeboat was lost in
a storm in 1883.

Unravelling

We are the new women.
We wouldn't be seen dead
knitting.

We make up our lives
to our own patterns:
they are intricate

and ambitious,
bold and original,
coats of many colours.

But oh the hours of unpicking,
trying to get back
to where they went wrong.

Vicki Feaver

Being a Student

(Fourth Week, First Year)

Unless you become the eternal kind
It lasts three years; time
To get married, divorced,
Re-married, or for Christ's ministry.

Standing-water time. Time
So much wanted that
When it comes, you can't believe
That it's here. Am I truly

That godlike thing? Do junior
School kids, seeing me, think
Student, the way they recognize
A blackbird, the way I did?

The feeling hasn't arrived yet.
Inside I'm still last year's
Sixth-former, pretending. At home they'd see
Through my jeans and leg-warmers

To the uniform self, caged
Between O and A. Here I'm defined
By last year's crop. The cleaner
Thinks I'll turn out like the girl

Who had this room before. *Easy
Meat*! she says, and sucks
Her cheeks, investigating the waste-paper
Basket for signs of sin.

My spelling mistakes are old
Friends to my new tutor. He keeps
Calling me *Mandy*, too. He sees
Three or four of me, cloudily.

And all the time the great
Term revolves, like the gerbils'
Wheel at home, and light falls
In unique patterns each day

On the sea and the fell,
And none of it comes again ever,
So rich, so wild, so fast,
While inside me I haven't

Even arrived here yet.

U. A. Fanthorpe

The Genie in the Jar

(for Nina Simone)

take a note and spin it around spin it around
don't
prick your finger
take a note and spin it around
on the Black loom on the Black loom
careful baby
don't prick your finger

take the air and weave the sky
around the Black loom around the Black loom
make the sky sing a Black song sing a blue song
sing my song make the sky sing a Black song
from the Black loom from the Black loom
careful baby
don't prick your finger

take a genie and put her in a jar
put her in a jar
wrap the sky around her
take the genie and put her in a jar
wrap the sky around her
listen to her sing
sing a Black song our Black song
from the Black loom
singing to me
from the Black loom
careful baby
don't prick your finger

Nikki Giovanni

Scarecrow

the scarecrow
looks sad tonight all covered in rags
her solitude made of sticks
flapping in the dark field
and her eyes that won't shut
watching the cows at sleep.
with no shoes
and wind in her pockets,
she counts those stars
she can see
from her fixed angle
and listens to the black sticks rubbing
as she spits her curses at the moon.

Stef Pixner

A Post Card from Greece

The sun over here makes us browner,
after the burning wears off;
this blue kind of water is warmer
and waves are never as rough.

The flowers that grow here are brighter,
we stay up much later, to eat;
white-painted houses are whiter,
the coffee is thicker, and sweet.

With sand in my undies,
cheese in the salad
and a hole in the bathroom floor,

with beds that feel harder
and days that seem longer
with things to be looking for

like donkeys and tortoises,
cats and cooked octopuses
and wine in the water to drink,

with castles on mountains
and thousands of candles
I like it in Greece, I think.

Jane Whittle

Holiday Girls

'*British Holiday Girls in Death Crash*' – *newspaper headline*

Let Beryl Cook paint this triptych. First,
the Setting Out from Victoria. Laden
with overnight bags and make-up cases,
they jostle on to the train. Their summer dresses
patterned with daisies, shoulders bare
in expectation of bronze, their 'natural' perms
guaranteed to last through swimming-pool and disco,
mark them out from the business crowd.
That guard at the gate with his back toward us:
is that a hand of bones stretched out
to take the ticket? Too late to look now.

The middle panel, the Death Crash, should show
a blackened plain under a bloody sky,
and strewn on the plain, in tender enumeration,
squashed lipsticks, bottles oozing white pulp
of lotions, Instamatics, Mars bars,
Mills and Boon romances, and the Holiday Girls:
the legs of one sticking out from under
some piece of machinery, the other seen
in outline only, under the ambulance sheet.

88

And last, the Arrival at Butlin's, Death-on-Sea.
A three-piece band of tuxedoed angels strikes up:
their haloes are inscribed 'Kiss Me Quick' and 'You've
    Had It'.
Down from the neon-lit Pleasure Pavilion pours
the army of saints and martyrs, displaying
the symbols and instruments of their suffering:
Auntie May with her surgical stockings, Uncle Ted
with his X-ray plates, and cousin George,
clutching the steering shaft that went through his
    chest.
And after them, the Thousand Virgins (half a dozen
will do, we must imagine the rest),
each one a Miss Lovely Legs, and, in their midst,
holding a tray of rock cakes, our Heavenly Mum.

Now let the eye travel upward. Be bold, Mrs Cook,
to paint what the heart of the poor has always
    known:
the Son setting out the cups and saucers for tea,
the Father in braces and rolled-up trousers
coming up from the sea, and a shimmering bird
nourished by no earthly cuttlefish, spreading its wings
over the strapless shoulders and permanent curls
of the laugh-a-minute, whew-what-a-scorcher,
British death-crash, sic-transit-Bank-Holiday-Monday,
Holiday Girls.

Vicki Raymond

Things

There are worse things than having behaved foolishly
   in public.
There are worse things than these miniature betrayals,
committed or endured or suspected; there are worse
   things
than not being able to sleep for thinking about them.
It is 5 a.m. All the worse things come stalking in
and stand icily about the bed looking worse and worse
   and worse.

Fleur Adcock

Anno Wreck Sick

I am Anorexic   I mean
I really think thin   real lean   I
mean I've been carried away to
the point where
I've all but disappeared.

Poor virgin, poor maiden I was – oh
they wanted me fed up plump, firm, fair oh
so femininely fattened for the
rutting rites – they wanted my sweet flesh
to be some sacrifice on
the altarbed of adulthood.

Anno Wreck Sick – I could
play around with the hollow sound
play frantic antics with semantics but
that's not what you want to know   oh no   let's
get right down to the nitty, dig to the dying bone
search in my shrinking skull
the meaty matter of it.

So you want to know why I don't
want to grow   oh please think of what it –
sweet sixteen get preened for prodding, fumbling
grunting, mumbling while small child me inside
dies crumbling.

Scars will heal
Shrink and heal
Shrink my head
I wanna be dead.

Cut off your bloody nose, my ma
always said, to spite, she said
oh ma, how right, how right.

Please don't pin my body, man
lovely living butterfly, please
don't try, I'd sooner
die.

So I'll waste the flesh away, ruin
your chances, forestall
your advances.

Anorexic, that's what I am,
happy to be carried away
with a skinny laugh
to my sweet deathbed.

Magi Gibson

The Fat Black Woman's Motto on Her Bedroom Door

IT'S BETTER TO DIE IN THE FLESH OF HOPE
THAN TO LIVE IN THE SLIMNESS OF DESPAIR

Grace Nichols

The Fat Lady's Request

I, too, will disappear, will
Escape into centuries of darkness.

Come here and give me a cuddle,
Sit on my lap and give me a hug

While we are both still enjoying
This mysterious whirling planet.

And if you find me fat, you find me
Also, easy to find, very easy to find.

Joyce la Verne

The Concerned Adolescent

Our planet spins around the sun
in its oval-shaped orbit
like a moth circling a bright, hot, golden-yellow light bulb.
Look at this beautiful, lovely
blue and green and white jewel
shining against the dark black sky.
It is doomed.

On another planet somewhere far away in the galaxy
beings are discussing the problems of Earth.
'It is a wonderful world,' says their leader,
'It has roaring oceans filled with many kinds of fishes,
It has green meadows bedecked with white and yellow
    flowers,
Its trees have twisting roots and fruitful, abundant
    branches.
But it is doomed.

'The problem with this lovely, beautiful world, you see,
Is the inhabitants, known as HUMAN BEINGS.
Human beings will not live in peace and love
and care for the little helpless creatures who share the
    planet with them.
They pollute the world, they kill and eat the animals.
Everywhere there is blood and the stench of death.
Human beings make war and hate one another.
They do not understand their young, they reject their ideals
they make them come home early from the disco.
They are doomed.'

Soon a great explosion, a terrible cloud
will wipe out all the life on this planet,
including those people who do not see how important
    my poem is.
They are certainly doomed.

Wendy Cope

Mollie Haggarty

Poor old Mollie Haggarty
Ate chops when they were maggoty.
Now her conscience can't decide –
Did she commit insecticide?

Dorothy Barnham

Rules for Beginners

They said: 'Honour thy father and thy mother.
Don't spend every evening at the Disco.
Listen to your teachers, take an O level
or two. Of course, one day you'll have children.
We've tried our best to make everything nice.
Now it's up to you to be an adult!'

She went to all the 'X' films like an adult.
Sometimes she hung around the Mecca Disco.
Most of the boys she met were dead O level,
smoking and swearing, really great big children.
She had a lot of hassle with her mother;
it was always her clothes or her friends that weren't
    nice.

At school some of the teachers were quite nice,
but most of them thought they were minding
    children,
although they said – 'Now, Susan, you're an adult,
behave like one.' The snobs taking O level
never had fun, never went to the Disco;
they did their homework during 'Listen with Mother'.

She said: 'I'd hate to end up like my mother,
but there's this lovely bloke down at the Disco
who makes me feel a lot more like an adult.'
He murmured – 'When I look at you, it's nice
all over! Can't you cut out that O level
scene? Christ, I could give you twenty children!'

He had to marry her. There were three children
– all girls. Sometimes she took them to her mother
to get a break. She tried to keep them nice.
It was dull all day with kids, the only adult.
She wished they'd told you that, instead of O level.
Sometimes she dragged her husband to the Disco.

She got a part-time job at the Disco,
behind the bar; a neighbour had the children.
Now she knew all about being an adult
and honestly it wasn't very nice.
Her husband grumbled – 'Where's the dinner,
    mother?'
'I'm going down the night-school for an O level,

I am,' said mother. 'Have fun at the Disco,
kids! When you're an adult, life's all O level.
Stay clear of children, keep your figures nice!'

Carol Rumens

97

The Way We Live

Pass the tambourine, let me bash out praises
to the Lord God of movement, to Absolute
non-friction, flight, and the scary side:
death by avalanche, birth by failed contraception.
Of chicken tandoori and reggae, loud, from
      tenements,
commitment, driving fast and unswerving
friendship. Of T-shirts on pulleys, giros and Bombay,
barmen, dreaming waitresses with many fake-gold
bangles. Of airports, impulse, and waking to
      uncertainty,
to strip-lights, motorways, or that pantheon –
the mountains. To overdrafts and grafting

and the fir slow pulse of wipers as you're
creeping over Rannoch, while the God of moorland
walks abroad with his entourage of freezing fog,
his bodyguard of snow.
Of endless gloaming in the North, of Asiatic swelter,
to launderettes, anecdotes, passions and exhaustion,
Final Demands and dead men, the skeletal grip
of government. To misery and elation; mixed,
the sod and caprice of landlords.
To the way it fits, the way it is, the way it seems
to be: let me bash out praises – pass the tambourine.

Kathleen Jamie

98

Son

Coming home from the women-only bar,
I go into my son's room.
He sleeps – fine, freckled face
thrown back, the scarlet lining of his mouth
shadowy and fragrant, his small teeth
glowing dull and milky in the dark,
opal eyelids quivering
like insect wings, his hands closed
in the middle of the night.
                              Let there be enough
room for this life: the head, lips,
throat, wrists, hips, sex,
knees, feet. Let no part go
unpraised. Into any new world we enter, let us
take this man.

Sharon Olds

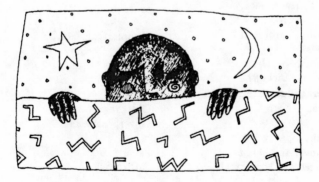

Index of Authors

Acknowledgements

The editor and publishers gratefully acknowledge the following for permission to reproduce copyright poems in this book:

'For Heidi with Blue Hair' by Fleur Adcock from *The Incident Book* by Fleur Adcock, published by the Oxford University Press, 1986, copyright © Fleur Adcock, 1986, reprinted by permission of the publisher; 'Things' by Fleur Adcock from *Selected Poems* by Fleur Adcock, published by the Oxford University Press, 1983, copyright © Fleur Adcock, 1983, reprinted by permission of the publisher; 'Phenomenal Woman' by Maya Angelou from *And Still I Rise* by Maya Angelou, copyright © Maya Angelou, 1978, reprinted by permission of Random House, Inc. & Virago Press; 'The Nature Lesson' by Marjorie Baldwin from *The Slain Unicorn and Other Poems* by Marjorie Baldwin, published by Outposts Publications, London, copyright © Marjorie Baldwin, 1965, reprinted by permission of the author; 'Mollie Haggarty' by Dorothy Barnham from *More Stuff and Nonsense* edited by Michael Dugan and published by Collins, Sydney, 1974, copyright © Dorothy Barnham; 'Indian Children Speak' by Juanita Bell, first published by Vintage Books, New York, copyright © Juanita Bell; 'Peck's Bad Boys' by Judi Benson, first published in *The Rialto*, No. 15, Winter 1989-90 edited by Michael Mackmin and John Wakeman, copyright © Judi Benson, 1989, reprinted by permission of the author; 'A Happy Childhood' by Eulalia Bernard, translated by Amanda Hopkinson, first published by the Women's Press, English translation copyright © Amanda Hopkinson, 1989, reprinted by permission of the translator; 'Vestment' by Ana Blandiana, translated by Peter Jay and Anca Cristofovici from *The Hour of Sand*, published by the Anvil Press Poetry Ltd, copyright © Peter Jay and Anca Cristofovici, 1990, reprinted by permission of Peter Jay; 'Yuh Hear Bout?' by Valerie Bloom, first published by Bogle-Overture Publications Ltd, copyright © Valerie Bloom, reprinted by permission of J. Huntley for and on behalf of Valerie Bloom; 'shopping' by Jenny Boult from *About Auntie Rose*, published by Omnibus, copyright © Jenny Boult, 1988, reprinted by permission of the author; 'natural high' and 'school days' by Jean Binta Breeze, copyright © Jean Binta Breeze; 'Space-age Lover' by Jennifer Brice from *Purple and Green*, published by Rivelin Grapheme Press, copyright © Jennifer Brice; 'A Short Note on Schoolgirls' by Alison Campbell, copyright © Alison Campbell; 'Loch, Black Rock, Beautiful Boat' by Meg Campbell, first published by Te Kotare Press, New Zealand, copyright © Meg Campbell, 1981; 'The Class Game' by Mary Casey, copyright © Mary Casey; 'Please Give This Seat to an Elderly or Disabled Person' by Nina Cassian from *Life Sentence*, 1990, published by the Anvil Press Poetry Ltd, copyright © Nina Cassian, 1990, reprinted by permission of the publisher; 'Blind Girl' by Jane Cooper from *Scaffolding*, 1984, published by the Anvil Press Poetry Ltd, copyright © Jane Cooper, 1984, reprinted by permission of the publisher; 'The Concerned Adolescent' by Wendy Cope from *PBS Anthology*, 1990, copyright © Wendy Cope, 1987, reprinted by permission of the author; 'Magnetic' by Wendy Cope from *Does She Like Word-Games*, published by Anvil Press Limited Edition, 1988, copyright © Wendy Cope, 1986, reprinted by permission of the author; 'The Name of the Game' by Jenny Craig from *The Beaver Book of School Verse* edited by Jennifer Curry and published by The Hamlyn Publishing Group, copyright © Jennifer Curry, 1981, reprinted by permission of Jennifer Curry; 'The Royal Grammar School, Newcastle' and 'Short Thought' by Elaine Cusack from *Bossy Parrot*, 1987, published by Bloodaxe Books, copyright © Elaine Cusack, 1987, reprinted by permission of the author; 'Sweet Sixteen' by Eunice de Souza, copyright © Eunice de Souza; 'The Women of Mumbles Head' by Maura Dooley from *Ivy Leaves and Arrows*, published by Bloodaxe Books, copyright © Maura Dooley, 1987, reprinted by permission of the author; 'Lovesick' by Carol Ann Duffy, published by the Anvil Press, 1987, copyright © Carol Ann Duffy, 1987, reprinted by permission of the author; 'Valentine' by Carol Ann Duffy, copyright © Carol Ann Duffy, 1992, printed by permission of the author; 'Being a Student' and 'Women Laughing' by U. A. Fanthorpe from *Voices Off*, published by Peterloo Poets, 1984, copyright © U. A. Fanthorpe, 1984, reprinted by permission of the publisher; 'Unravelling' by Vicki Feaver, which first appeared in the *Observer* 'Clean Sheets', 1981, copyright © Vicki Feaver, 1981, reprinted by permission of the author; 'I am Happy' by Delfy Gochez Fernandez, translated by Amanda Hopkinson, published by the Women's Press, 1989, translation copyright © Amanda Hopkinson, 1989, reprinted by permission of the translator; 'Song (October 1969)' by Kath Fraser, copyright © Kath Fraser; 'Anno Wreck Sick' by

Toughie Toffee, published by Collins, 1989, copyright © Irene Rawnsley, 1989, reprinted by permission of the author; 'Chat Show' by Vicki Raymond from *Small Arm Practice*, published by William Heinemann, Australia, copyright © Vicki Raymond, reprinted by permission of the author; 'Holiday Girls' by Vicki Raymond, published in *Island* magazine, copyright © Vicki Raymond, reprinted by permission of the author; 'Rules for Beginners' by Carol Rumens, published by Chatto & Windus, copyright © Carol Rumens, reprinted by permission of the publisher; 'Disabled Swimmers' Night' and 'Piccadilly Line' by Carole Satyamurti from *Changing the Subject* by Carole Satyamurti, published by the Oxford University Press, 1990, copyright © Carole Satyamurti, 1990, reprinted by permission of the publisher; 'For an Unborn Baby' by Janet Shepperson from *Trio 5*, published by Blackstaff Press, 1987, copyright © Janet Shepperson, 1987, reprinted by permission of the publisher; 'Latch-key Child' by Valerie Sinason first published in *Inkstains and Stilettos*, 1988, by Headland, copyright © Valerie Sinason, 1988, reprinted by permission of the author; 'To the Spider in the Crevice Behind the Toilet Door' by Janet Sutherland, copyright © Janet Sutherland; 'Didactica Nova' by Grete Tartler, translated by B. Walker and A. Deletant from *Silent Voices*, published by Forest, 1986, translation copyright © Brenda Walker and Andrea Deletant, 1986, reprinted by permission of the translators; 'Advice to a Teenage Daughter' by Isobel Thrilling from *Ultrasonics of Snow*, published by Rivelin-Grapheme, 1985, copyright © Isobel Thrilling, 1985, reprinted by permission of the author; 'Remember' by Alice Walker from *Horses Make the Landscape More Beautiful* by Alice Walker, published by The Women's Press, copyright © Alice Walker, reprinted by permission of David Higham Associates; 'A Post Card from Greece' by Jane Whittle from *Around the World in 80 Poems* edited by Jennifer and Graeme Curry and published by Hutchinson Children's Books, copyright © Jane Whittle, reprinted by permission of the publisher; 'We Can Always' by Nellie Wong, first published by Kelsey Street Press, California, copyright © Nellie Wong.

Every effort has been made to trace copyright holders, but in a few cases this has proved impossible. The editor and publishers apologize for these cases of unwilling copyright transgression and would like to hear from any copyright holders not acknowledged.

LaVergne, TN USA
08 July 2010
188828LV00001B/78/P